MINOR II V MASTERY
FOR GUITAR

Learn Bebop Soloing on the Minor II V I Sequence for Jazz Guitar

JOSEPH ALEXANDER

FUNDAMENTAL CHANGES

Minor ii V Mastery for Jazz Guitar

Learn Bebop Soloing on the Minor II V I Sequence for Jazz Guitar

ISBN: 978-1-78933-047-2

Published by **www.fundamental-changes.com**

Copyright © 2019 Joseph Alexander

The moral right of this author has been asserted.

www.fundamental-changes.com

Twitter: @guitar_joseph

Over 10,000 fans on Facebook: **FundamentalChangesInGuitar**

Instagram: **FundamentalChanges**

For over 350 Free Guitar Lessons with Videos Check Out

www.fundamental-changes.com

Cover Image Copyright: Shutterstock: Adobe Stock

Contents

Introduction

It's been over a year since I wrote my first Fundamental Changes book on the Major ii V I progression. In that time I've been astonished by the kind comments and positive reviews that I have received, especially when I get the occasional heartfelt letter from someone relating to the personal challenges documented in the introduction. All I ever set out to do was to write a straightforward, step by step process of learning jazz improvisation, so I'm touched by the response. Thank you.

Among the emails I get, I am often asked when the follow up will be available. A lot of people asked for a book that applied my thinking process to the minor ii V i (two, five, one) progression. It's taken me a year, but it's finally here.

The theory will come later, but suffice to say that the minor ii V i is a very different beast to the major ii V I, as it can be treated in a variety of different ways. It can be seen as a combination of many different scales, so there really are a multitude of approaches that can be applied to improvisation on its structure.

I will always stick to my 'first choice' soloing approaches so as not to weigh the reader down in cumbersome theory. As with my first jazz book I will help you to build your solo lines from the ground up, focusing on the most fundamental skill in jazz/bebop playing: the solid understanding and application of appropriate arpeggios and bebop scales.

As I have mentioned, the theory can sometimes get a little complicated so I'll always summarise a concept before launching into an in-depth explanation. This way you can get straight to the music if you want to skip the theory.

Finally, I recommend reading my first book, **Fundamental Changes in Jazz Guitar** before diving into this one. Many of the concepts here are discussed at a more basic 'building block' level.

Get the Audio

The audio files for this book are available to download for free from www.fundamental-changes.com. The link is in the top right-hand corner. Simply select this book title from the drop-down menu and follow the instructions to get the audio.

We recommend that you download the files directly to your computer, not to your tablet, and extract them there before adding them to your media library. You can then put them on your tablet, iPod or burn them to CD. On the download page there is a help PDF and we also provide technical support via the contact form.

For over 350 Free Lessons with Videos Check out:

www.fundamental-changes.com

Over 10,000 fans on Facebook: **FundamentalChangesInGuitar**

Instagram: **FundamentalChanges**

How to Learn Jazz Guitar Soloing

The guitar can be a complicated instrument to learn. Not only do we have to learn the same scales, arpeggios and chords as other instruments, we often end up learning each scale in many different fingering permutations. This, in itself, is a lot of work and while of great importance, it can distract from our main objective: making music.

Music is about sounds not fretboard fingerings, so the way I teach jazz guitar is to first focus on only one fretboard position in one key. Think about it: an octave in music really is quite a big distance. Two octaves is huge. In one position on the guitar we can easily cover two octaves. If your audience has their eyes closed, how many would know that you're playing in position?

While complete fluency all over the fretboard is our long-term goal, I believe that we should always train our ears first and worry about the idiosyncrasies of our instrument later. Our primary goal is to make and play music as soon as possible, and removing the distraction of learning multiple shapes helps us to do just that.

Once you're familiar with the concepts and sounds in this book, *please* explore other positions and keys on your guitar. There is some guidance about this in the final chapter with some recommendations.

Finally, *play* this stuff! Find some jazz standard backing tracks on YouTube, or even better, form a band! This is the scary, bit but if you're with the right people there is no negative judgment, just positive re-enforcement. Plus it's fun and will teach you more than I ever can in any book. There is a list of tunes in the book that make great use of the minor ii V i progression. Learn them.

If in doubt trust your ears.

Have fun and remember, if you're too scared to play a wrong note, you're not really pushing yourself ;-)

All the audio examples in this book are available for *free* download from

www.fundamental-changes.com/audio-downloads

Understanding the Minor ii V i Progression

The *minor ii V i* chord progression is seen by jazz musicians as deriving from the Harmonic Minor Scale. However, as with many things in music, there are a few *standard* alterations that are often used to make things sound a little sweeter to western ears.

If you have read my first book, **Fundamental Changes in Jazz Guitar**, you will know that this chord progression is called a 'ii V I' because we are using the 2nd, 5th and 1st chords from the harmonised scale. In this case we use the harmonised Harmonic *Minor* scale – hence *minor* ii V i.

To explain this further and make the concept much clearer, let's take a look at the chord theory behind the minor ii V I chord progression in terms of the Harmonic Minor scale.

Here is the scale of D Harmonic Minor:

Example 1a

D Harmonic Minor Scale

Play through this scale and get a feel for its sound. It is the basis of the minor ii V i. Now we can harmonise (build chords on) the 2nd, 5th and 1st notes of the scale:

Example 1b

The chord diagrams at the top of the line are not identical to the notation, but they are good guitar voicings for the chords that we form.

The harmonised 2nd (ii) degree of the D Harmonic Minor scale (E) forms a *minor 7b5* chord which can be played like this on the guitar:

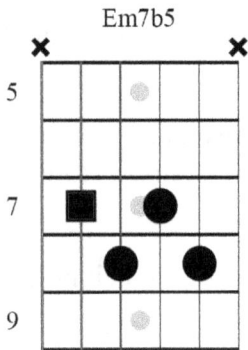

Em7b5

The chord built on the first (i) note (degree) of the scale is a *minor / major 7* chord. You may not have been familiar with this chord until now, but you can think of it as a three note minor triad (D F A) with a *major* or *natural* 7th note added (C#).

It can be played like this:

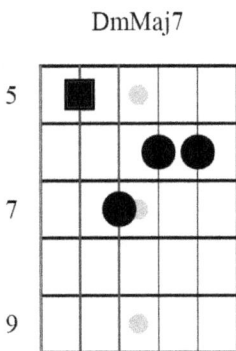

DmMaj7

(Fingering, bass note to top = 1, 4, 2, 3)

The V or *dominant* chord is A7 and for now we will use this useful barre chord form:

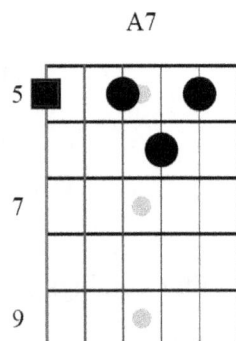

A7

When we use these chords in the minor ii V I progression we get the chord sequence shown in here.

Example 1c

This is a minor ii V i in its purest form. To give it its full description, the chord progression is

ii(m7b5) – V(7) – i(min/maj7)

This is quite a mouthful, so we normally just use the phrase 'minor ii V i' to describe the above sequence. Notice that for ii and i we use *lower case* roman numerals. It is the convention in music to use lower case to denote minor-type chords and upper case to denote major type chords, hence 'V7' *not* 'v7'.

When you play through this chord progression, do you notice that the Dmin/Maj7 chord sounds tense and quite unresolved? Normally the tonic chord in a progression acts as a kind of musical full stop, but the inherent tension in the min/Maj7 chord does not really allow for this.

Often musicians do not use the min/Maj chord as a resolution point in a chord progression. You *do* see the min/Maj7 chord used, but if I were to guess I'd say that it is only used about 20% of the time. The majority of minor ii V i chord progressions will normally substitute a 'straight' minor or minor 7 chord for the tonic min/ Maj7 chord.

This presents us with a couple of small soloing challenges which will be discussed later, but for now the minor ii V i chord progression we will study in this book is this:

Example 1d

One notable composition that *does* use the min/Maj7 chord as a resolution to a minor ii V i progression is *Solar* by Miles Davies. The voicing of the D minor 7 chord in the above example is this:

The soloing challenges I have mentioned all revolve around the fact that the final D minor 7 chord does *not* come from the same 'parent' D Harmonic Minor scale that the ii and V chords derived from. (If you remember, we were expecting a min/Maj7 chord).

This means that we may have to adjust our thinking slightly when we are soloing over the Dm7 chord. All this will be covered in later chapters and is an important part of the minor ii V i sound.

For now, make sure you are able to play the chords along with backing track one.

Start by playing each chord on beat one of the bar.

Then try playing on beat 1 and 3 of each bar.

You can also play on just beat 2 and beat 4 of each bar.

Finally, try playing the following rhythm to make the music come alive:

Example 1e

Before moving on to the next chapter, make sure you can change cleanly between the chords in time with the slow, medium and fast backing tracks.

The Basics of Minor ii V i Soloing

A big mistake many guitarists make is to approach bebop improvisation from the basis of scalic playing. The early jazz language developed on marching instruments such as trumpets, trombones and clarinets. These instruments are extremely adept at playing fast musical lines based around arpeggios, so to develop a proper understanding and aural awareness of the genre, bebop should be always approached from the perspective of arpeggios, not scales.

Later, we will use scales to 'fill in the gaps' but it is essential for now that our musical concepts and vocabulary are built from a solid foundation of arpeggios.

It is fair to say that many bebop solos are formed from appropriate arpeggios with the gaps filled in with scale tones and chromatic approach notes. Unfortunately for us as guitarists, arpeggios are trickier to play than scales on our instrument. This is one of the challenges we must overcome on our way to learning the jazz language. The shapes will become comfortable more quickly than you think, so I would encourage you to go slowly and persevere with any arpeggio fingerings that you might initially find awkward.

What is an Arpeggio?

An arpeggio is the notes of a chord played sequentially instead of simultaneously. You are probably familiar with the concept of naming chord tones in terms of *root, 3rd, 5th and 7th*. They are named like this because of the way we form chords by 'skipping' notes from a parent scale.

We will begin by learning the appropriate arpeggios that fit over each successive chord in the minor ii V i progression.

Over the E minor7b5 (Em7b5) chord, we play an Em7b5 arpeggio. (Formula 1 b3 b5 b7)

Over the A7 chord, we play an A7 Arpeggio. (Formula 1 3 5 b7)

Over the Dm7 chord, we play a Dm7 arpeggio. (Formula 1 b3 5 b7)

In notation, these arpeggios can be played in the following way:

Example 2a, Em7b5 Arpeggio:

Em7b5 Arpeggio

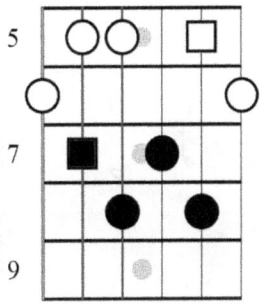

Notice that the solid dots in the arpeggio shape form the Em7b5 chord that you learned in the previous chapter. The notation in the tablature above begins on the square root note, E. For now you do not need to play the two lowest pitched notes in the neck diagram.

Example 2b, A7 Arpeggio:

A7 Arpeggio

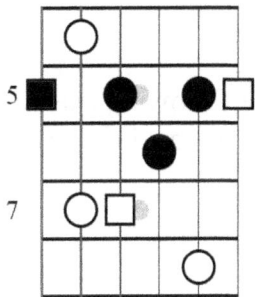

Again, here the solid dots are from the A7 chord you learned previously

Example 2c, Dm7 Arpeggio:

Dm7 Arpeggio

Once again, you will see that the solid dots are the chord shape you have already learned, and the arpeggio notes are built around that shape. Begin on the square root note and ignore the notes on the bass string for now.

Let's start by getting familiar with the chord to arpeggio relationship. Play the chord as shown by the solid dots and then play the related arpeggio. Do this with all three chords.

Remember, arpeggios are just the notes of the chord played consecutively.

When you are close to having all three arpeggios memorised around each chord, try the following exercise with backing track 1. We are going to play *just* the root of each chord/arpeggio while the backing track is playing.

Exercise 2d

While this exercise may seem simplistic at first, knowing and hearing where your root is, is absolutely essential when it comes to confident soloing. Notice that for the second bar of Dm7 I have played the higher octave of the D root. Try this idea with each bar in the following manner:

Exercise 2e

Play this again this with the notes in each bar reversed, so you are playing the higher octave root first. In this position, there are root notes over three octaves in the A7 arpeggio. Can you find them?

Moving on, we will now repeat the exercise but add in the *3rd* of each arpeggio:

Exercise 2f

Again, reverse the note sequences in each bar so that you play the 3rd first, then the root. Next, play the same intervals in the higher octave.

Exercise 2g

Remember to reverse the notes here as well so you play the higher octave 3rd and *then* the root.

Exercises like these are extremely important in teaching you how to begin your lines from notes other than the root, they increase your vision and aural awareness on the guitar.

Next we add in the 5th to the root and 3rd:

Exercise 2h

Once again, practice reversing the order of the notes in each bar so you play the intervals 5th, 3rd, root, and then repeat both exercises in the higher octave.

Finally, we will play all four notes of each arpeggio, the root, 3rd, 5th and 7th.

Exercise 2i

Em7♭5   **A7**   **Dm7**

(musical notation and guitar tablature)

Play these patterns in the higher octave too and if you run out of notes, just double back on yourself. Remember to practice each bar descending from the 7th of each chord:

Exercise 2j

Em7♭5   **A7**   **Dm7**

(musical notation and guitar tablature)

The ability to play the appropriate arpeggio over each chord is a huge step on the way to mastering any bebop progression. Not only are your guitar skills improving, your ears are improving too.

Look at this stage as learning where the strong notes of the progression lie. If you can always hear them and find them on your guitar you will always be able to resolve any line that you are playing if you trust your ears.

Practice these ideas with all three of the minor ii V i backings tracks (in D minor) – slow, medium and fast. This will increase your competence and technical ability. As your confidence grows, switch back to the slowest backing track and master the following challenges:

- Just play the 3rd of each chord. (Master this in the lower octave, then in a higher octave, then both)

- Just play the 7th of each chord

- Just play the 5th of each chord

- Play the 3rd and then the 7th (first in low octave then in high octave. Finally, play both notes together as a chord)

- Play the 7th and then the 3rd

- Play the arpeggio tones in the order 3, 5, 7, 1

- Play the arpeggio tones in the order 5, 7, 1, 3

- Play the arpeggio tones in the order 7, 1, 3, 5

- Play the arpeggio tones in the order 7, 5, 3, 1

- Play the arpeggio tones in the order 3, 1, 7, 5

Don't move on to the next chapter until you are very comfortable with at least the first five exercises in the above list. The following example is the answer to challenge one in the lower octave, but I have deliberately not given you the answers to the rest. This is to help you independently improve your vision, aural skills and fretboard awareness.

Although this may seem difficult at first, stay with it and treat the challenges as 'tough love'. Some time spent here will pay exponential dividends for the rest of your jazz guitar playing life.

Exercise 2k

Hitting the Changes with Arpeggio Connections

In the previous chapter we studied how to use appropriate arpeggios to *outline* the chord progression we were soloing over. Each time we began from the same pre-defined arpeggio tone on each chord, for example the 3rd of Em7b5, the 3rd of A7 and then the 3rd of Dm7. This is an extremely important skill to practice because it teaches us where the strong, resolved arpeggio tones are for each chord. Practicing in this way, however, does force us to jump about on the neck whenever the chord changes.

We will now study how to join arpeggios together using the 'closest available tone' concept. Instead of jumping to a pre-defined note when the chord changes, we will now move to the closest note in the new arpeggio.

Study **Example 3a**

This line begins by ascending the Em7b5 arpeggio from the root. When the chord changes to A7, instead of jumping to the root of A7, I move to the closest note of the A7 arpeggio – in this case, the 3rd (C#).

From there I continue the ascent and when it is time to change to Dm7, I again aim for the closest note in the Dm7 arpeggio (F), which is located on the 6th fret, second string. To finish, I descend the Dm7 arpeggio.

This is just one of a multitude of permutations we have available when changing chords. For example, when it is time to change to the A7 arpeggio, there is no need for me to continue ascending in pitch.

Example 3b

In this example I begin the same way and change into the A7 arpeggio in the same place, but I then *descend* the A7 arpeggio creating a completely new bebop line. As the chord changes to Dm7, I move up from the *5th* of the A7 chord into the *b3rd* of the Dm7 arpeggio. This semitone movement is extremely strong melodically. Try playing the previous two examples with and without a backing track. You should still be able to internally *hear* the chords change, even when the backing track isn't playing.

Of course, we can start from any point in the arpeggio. The next line starts from the *b3rd* of the Em7b5 chord.

Example 3c

Do you notice how I can use a melodic sequence and *still* target the closest arpeggio tone as each chord changes?

Here's another line ascending from the same place:

Example 3d

The above line ascends from the *b3* of Em7b5 and targets the *b7* of A7 before resolving to the *b3* of D minor.

Our lines can begin with descending ideas too as shown in here.

Example 3e

Example 3e descends from the *b5* of the Em7b5 chord, hits the *3rd* of A7 and resolves upwards with a semitone step into the *b3* of Dm7. When changing to Dm7, I could have landed on the root of the chord, but landing on the root on beat one of the final chord can be a bit of a brick wall when it comes to building momentum in your solo. It is often better to aim for a different arpeggio tone as it will give more forward energy to the melodic line.

Take a few days to let your fingers wander around the arpeggio shapes, always looking for the closest melodic link into the next chord.

The most efficient and effective way to explore how notes alter over chord changes is to divide the guitar up into two-string groups and practice soloing *only* using these groups. For example you can limit yourself to only using strings one and two, two and three, three and four, four and five or five and six.

Here are just a few permutations using only the first and second string:

Example 3f

Example 3g

Example 3h

Keep exploring these limited range ideas until you feel you have exhausted all the possibilities. Try repeating individual notes or using melodic patterns and jumps. Only when you can't think of any more ways to move between the closest tones on the chord change, move on to the second and third string group. Soon you will have every movement in this position memorised in your fingers and your ears.

As you gain more confidence through this procedure, practice with the three different tempo backing tracks. Also try the exercises with just a metronome to see if you can hear the chords change while only playing solo melody.

Notice that some of the arpeggio tones are *common* to two adjacent chords. You may want to avoid repeating the same note over a chord change at first, but later you will find that *common tones* can become a very strong and useful melodic device.

Chromatic Approach Notes

Chromatic approach notes really deserve an entire book to themselves. They form a massive topic and we can only really explore the tip of the iceberg here.

A crude explanation would be to say that, 'the melody notes that fall *on the strong beats* should be chord tones and the notes that fall *between* the strong beats should be scale tones or chromatic approach notes'.

While even the shallowest exploration of the previous statement will find it to be untrue in many circumstances, it is nevertheless a useful starting point to learn one of the most important concepts in bebop.

We will explore using *scale tones* in a later chapter, but for now let's examine the concept of inserting *chromatic approach notes* before rhythmically strong chord tones.

A chromatic approach note can be any melody note that approaches a target note by step. Chromatic approach notes are always *outside* the prevailing scale or harmony, but sometimes notes that are in the relevant scale are treated in the same way as chromatic approach notes.

Example 4a

On beat four of the first bar I have played the note C natural, which is a semitone below the C# I wish to target in bar two (C# is the 3rd of A7). This C natural has nothing to do with the prevailing harmony, yet because I place it on a *weak* part of the bar and resolve it to a *strong* arpeggio tone in bar two, it has an extremely melodic and pleasing effect on the line.

I can use the same concept as we move into bar three. Look at:

Example 4b

Again, I have placed a chromatic note on beat four of the bar. This time you could say the note is a true *chromatic passing note* because the melody between the A7 and Dm7 chords ascends G, G#, A.

It is completely acceptable that the chromatic passing note is taken from outside our key centre because it is played on a weak beat and resolves convincingly to a strong arpeggio tone in the following bar.

Example 4c is another chromatic idea that begins from the b3 of Em7b5 and uses an ascending chromatic passing note between each chord:

Chromatic notes don't have to be *between* the two notes in question. We can approach *any* arpeggio note from a semitone below as long as the chromatic note lies on a weak beat.

These notes are more accurately named *chromatic approach notes*. Exercise 4d is an example of a chromatic approach note from below.

24

As you can see, this line 'jumps' to a note one semitone below each of the first two chord changes. Again, as this occurs on a weak beat and resolves to a chord tone in the next bar, our ears accept the momentary dissonance. In bar three I use a *true* chromatic passing note to move into the second octave of the Dm7 arpeggio.

We can also approach a chord tone from a semitone above.

Exercise 4e:

Between bars one and two I use a chromatic approach note from below, but between bars two and three I use a chromatic approach note from above.

A great way to practice exploring chromatic approach note ideas is to play three 1/4 notes in the bar and then do an 1/8th note chromatic pattern on beat four. **Exercise 4f** demonstrates this idea using a concept known as boxing in:

As mentioned, chromatic approach notes are an extremely extensive topic but I've tried to show you some of the more common approaches to 'filling in the gaps' between chord changes. These ideas will be used repeatedly in this book and form a great deal of the bebop musical vocabulary.

As much as they are a melodic device, chromatic approach notes are also a rhythmic device that can be used to 'fill in a gap' between two adjacent notes, helping us to 'force' an arpeggio note onto a strong beat. We will examine this idea in later chapters.

Finally, let's study an extremely chromatic line which will give you an idea of just how far these concepts can be taken.

Example 4g

Instead of circling the notes that are chromatic alterations, this time I have highlighted only the chord tones. As you can see, the majority of the line is comprised of chromatic approach notes while still targeting the strong chord tones on most of the beats.

The first four notes of the previous exercise form a useful pattern called a 'double chromatic above, double chromatic below'. The target note on the Em7b5 is 'sandwiched' between two chromatic approach notes on each side.

Go through each bar in turn and 'extract' the chromatic ideas used. See if you can apply them to one chord. For example, try targeting every note of an A7 chord from a semitone below as shown on Dm7 in the last bar above. Don't worry about rhythm at this stage; just explore as many chromatic possibilities as you can.

Extended Arpeggios 3-9

One of the biggest innovations in the bebop period was to play arpeggios that did not begin from the root of the chord. Instead of playing from the root, jazz players often used arpeggios that began from the 3rd of the chord. By building a new four-note arpeggio from the 3rd of a chord, two things will happen:

1) We extend the arpeggio up to the *9th* of the chord/scale.

2) We avoid playing the root.

When we play the 9th of a chord we add richness and interest to our melodic line. This note can give our melodies more depth and help to take us away from basing our solos around only the notes in the chord we are playing over.

When we are playing in a band situation, it is normal for another instrument to be playing the root of the chord we are soloing on. However, even when we play unaccompanied guitar, our ears can magically fill in the gap in the harmonies when we don't include the root.

Play some of the lines in the previous chapter without a backing track. Even if you don't hit the bass note on the change, you can still *hear* the changes as you solo. Because of this, there is normally no real need for us to emphasise the root of a chord when we solo.

Forming 3 - 9 arpeggios

Study the following idea.

Example 5a

The first two bars show a D *natural* minor scale with the notes from the Dm7 arpeggio bracketed. This is how the arpeggio is *extracted* from the scale. We being on the root, skip the 2nd, play the 3rd, skip the 4th, etc. The arpeggio notes you have been playing in previous chapters are isolated in bar three.

In Example 5b, I have repeated exactly the same process, but this time I begin my four-note arpeggio from the b3 of the Dm7 (F).

Example 5b

By ascending four arpeggio notes from the F, my new arpeggio adds the note E (the 9th) and avoids the note D (the root).

We can form 3-9 extended arpeggios on any chord as long as we know which *parent* scale the chord belongs to. In this case we are using D Natural Minor as described in chapter three.

This is the fretboard diagram for our new 3-9 arpeggio:

Example 5c

As you can see, the 'D' root notes are included as triangles to help you learn this arpeggio around the original Dm7 chord, but *they are NOT played in this arpeggio!* Start the arpeggio from the note F using your 4th finger and begin by playing it from root to root. Learn to see it around the Dm7 chord next to it.

Learn this arpeggio over and around a static Dm7 chord (backing track 9). Get this important sound into your ears and try making music with it.

The same concept can be applied to the Em7b5 and A7 chords, although as you have learned, the notes in those chords derive from the D *Harmonic Minor* scale.

Look at the following

Example 5d

The first bar in Example 5d shows our original Em7b5 arpeggio. Compare this to the arpeggio shown in the second bar.

Can you see that I began on the note G (the b3) and continue up through the arpeggio? Both arpeggios have 3 notes in common, but this b3-b9 arpeggio now includes the note 'F' replacing the root E.

Example 5e shows the fingering diagram for this b3-b9 arpeggio:

Once again, the chord root (E) is shown as a square to help you tie this pattern to your original Em7b5 chord, but it is *not* played in this extended arpeggio. Start from the note G and learn the new arpeggio around the Em7b5 chord that is shown in the right-hand diagram. Practice this extended arpeggio over an Em7b5 vamp (backing track 8) to get the sound of the extended 'b9' note into your ears.

Finally, we will repeat the process with our V chord, the A7.

Example 5f

Here you will notice that the 9th in the extended arpeggio is flattened. You *may* have been expecting a natural 9 here, but as the A7 comes from the Harmonic Minor scale and not the major scale 'Mixolydian' chord that you may be used to, in this context Bb is the correct note.

Example 5g is the fretboard diagram of the full 3-b9 arpeggio:

This arpeggio, when not viewed in relation to the A7 chord is actually a Bb Diminished 7 arpeggio.

Playing a diminished 7 arpeggio on the 3rd of a dominant 7th chord is one of the most common substitutions in jazz. It will work over both major and minor ii V I progressions.

Soloing Using Extended Arpeggios

Now that we have learned how extended arpeggios are formed and played we will apply them to soloing on the minor ii V i progression.

I believe there are three clear stages when learning to solo with arpeggios over chord changes:

1) Begin arpeggios from a *set interval* each time. E.g., each arpeggio in turn begins from the 3rd or 7th etc.

2) Connect the arpeggios using the *closest note* concept. E.g., moving to the closest possible note in the next arpeggio

3) Connect the arpeggios using *chromatic approach notes* to fill in rhythmic gaps and to add melodic interest.

Targeting Specific Intervals on Chord Changes

Let us explore these stages using extended 3-9 arpeggios on the minor ii V i in D.

In Example 6a each extended arpeggio is played over each chord in turn beginning from the root. NB: when I say 'root', I mean the root of the *extended 3-9 arpeggio,* not the original chord.

Example 6a

It can help to learn these examples by first strumming a chord and then playing the associated 4-note extended arpeggio that goes with it. This will help you to strongly associate each melodic idea with the right chord shape.

Next try learning each arpeggio from the root *descending,* as shown in Example 6b:

Example 6b

Example 6c demonstrates the extended arpeggios played from 3-9:

Example 6c

Also learn this idea from the higher octave bass notes and descend the arpeggio.

Example 6d shows the extended arpeggios played from the 5th. Also learn this descending from the higher octave:

Example 6d

Finally, Example 6e plays from the *7th* of each extended arpeggio:

Example 6e

Once again, find the bass note in the higher octave and then descend through the arpeggio too.

Practice all these ideas with the slowest ii V i backing track, so that your ears can get used to the sound of these important extended arpeggio textures.

Targeting the Closest Change with Extended Arpeggios

When these extended arpeggio ideas become more natural under your fingers it is time to move on to hitting the closest note on each change. This is where the exercises start to sound more musical.

The following example begins from the 3rd of Em7b5 and plays up through the extended arpeggio (b3-b9). The closest note when the chord changes to A7 is the E (5th of A7). I then descend the extended arpeggio before resolving to the b3rd of Dm7.

Example 6f

The next example starts in the same way, but moves to the b7 of the A7 chord to create a new line.

Example 6g

In the following example, I link together descending shapes while switching to the closest note in each arpeggio as the chord changes.

In bar four I jump to the root D which I had been avoiding until this point. Notice how the resolution is extremely strong, almost like a brick wall in our melodic line.

Example 6h

The next example was created by limiting my playing to just the 3rd and 2nd strings. Once again, I am always aiming for the closest melodic change between chords.

Example 6i

This final example shows that you can use the closest note concept not just on the last note of each chord, but also on the first. Play through the following example and notice how I keep returning to the closest note *at the top* of the descending arpeggio.

Example 6j

In the previous example, the listener's ears will latch onto the first note of each bar and this kind of melodic idea can carry great strength in any solo.

Spend as much time as you can investigating these soloing permutations over the chord changes. You will return to this exercise for every new chord progression you come across while learning jazz guitar.

The quickest and most efficient method to learn to solo on new chord changes is to limit your playing to two-sting groups and explore every conceivable way to target arpeggio tones on chord changes.

As you get better at seeing and hearing the changes, progress to quicker backing tracks or start using 1/8th note lines.

Connecting Extended Arpeggios using Chromatic Approach Notes

As you become more familiar with the location of each target note, you need to start linking the extended arpeggios with chromatic approach notes, just as we did earlier in the book.

For the moment we will stay with 1/4 note rhythms as they really help you to develop your ears. If you stick with this approach you will eventually be able to automatically 'feel' and hear where the strong resolutions lie under your fingers. Also, these 1/4 note lines are very useful when the chord density is doubled.

For example, minor ii V i progressions often take place over just two bars instead of four as shown here.

Example 6k

This is the same line as Example 6j but this time played as 8th notes over two bars. It can be easy to develop bebop 1/8th note rhythms when we have the fundamental 1/4 note resolutions in our ears.

This should highlight the importance of sticking with the 1/4 note rhythms while learning these fundamental concepts. We will start looking at 1/8th note lines in the next chapter when we study bebop scales.

The following examples all use chromatic approach notes to target chord tones in the extended 3-9 arpeggios.

Example 7a

Example 7a targets the 5th of A7 from a semitone below and the 5th of Dm7 from a semitone below.

Example 7b

Example 7b uses chromatic passing notes into the b7 of A7 and the b3 of Dm7.

Example 7c

In Example 7c I 'box in' the 5th of A7 and then use the same technique to approach the 5th of Dm7

Example 7d

In Example 7d I 'box in' the 3rd of A7 and approach the 5th of Dm7 chromatically from below.

There are hundreds of ways to connect chord tones with chromatic approach notes, so setting some time aside each day to come up with new methods is always a worthy pursuit.

As long as you have a chord tone or extension (9th) on the beat you can't go far wrong. As you develop your ears and transcribe more solos by master improvisers, you will realise that you don't need a chord tone on *every* beat (some chromatic approach note patterns can be quite long). Trust your ears.

Always begin by learning chromatic approach note patterns as 1/4 note rhythms as we did in previous examples, but if you're eager to play them as 1/8th note bebop lines try playing them 'double time' over one of the 'quick changes' backing tracks.

The Phyrgian Dominant Bebop Scale

'Bebop' scales are eight-note scales created by adding a chromatic note to standard seven-note scales.

Bebop as a musical form revolves around fast groups of 1/8th notes. By using 8-note (octatonic) scales we can play long scalic runs which *automatically* keep the strong arpeggio tones on the beat.

In other words, because we have an *even* number of notes in the scale, when we start on a chord tone and play up or down in 1/8th notes, the other chord tones will automatically stay on the strong beats.

This can be seen in the following example with the Phrygian Dominant, and Phrygian Dominant 'Bebop' scales.

Let's look at the standard seven-note Phrygian Dominant scale in A. This is shown in two octaves here.

Example 8a

The arpeggio notes from the A7 chord are highlighted with brackets. Until the end of the first bar the arpeggio notes are all on strong beats (beats 1, 2, 3 and 4), but because this is a seven note scale, in the second octave, *all of the chord tones fall on the off-beats.*

As you know, this is extremely undesirable because all the strong arpeggio notes now fall in rhythmically weak parts of the bar.

The way we remedy this is to add a chromatic passing note between the b7 and the root. By adding this *natural 7* we have created an eight-note scale that will make the strong arpeggio tones fall on the strong beats of the bar.

The scale we create is the Phrygian Dominant Bebop Scale and it is one of the most important scales in jazz.

Example 8b

A Phrygian Dominant
Bebop

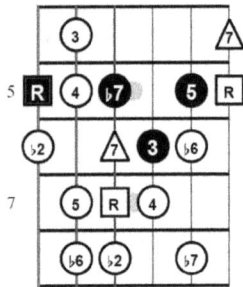

Examine the bracketed notes in Example 8b. Can you see how the extra note forces the arpeggio tones to always fall on a strong beat? In this example I started on the root of the scale, but the same is true *whichever* chord tone you begin on, and in *whatever direction* your melody moves.

For example, here is a line that descends two octaves from the 5th of A7 (E).

Example 8c

You can change direction at any point in the scale as long as you return to an arpeggio note on the beat.

Example 8d

I'm sure you're starting to see how useful the Phrygian Dominant Bebop scale can be over the V chord in a minor ii V i. The questions I have not addressed are *where* this scale comes from, and *why* it fits so perfectly in this musical context.

The minor ii V i progression is derived from the harmonised Harmonic Minor scale, so it is said that Harmonic Minor is our *parent* scale.

Despite having altered the final tonic chord to be a Dm7 instead of a Dmin/Maj7, the Harmonic Minor sound dominates the progression, especially over the first two chords.

While we *could* think about the Harmonic Minor scale when we are soloing, *most* jazz musicians will always view a ii V i progression from the point of view of the *dominant* (V) chord. The dominant chord, in our case A7, is simply a stronger musical sound and it is normally where the most of the harmonic and melodic tension will be in a progression.

The fifth mode of the Harmonic Minor scale is named the Phrygian Dominant and it will soon become natural for you to view the *whole* ii V i progression from the point of view of the Phrygian Dominant (Bebop) scale.

Em7b5/A = A7b9sus4

You may be wondering whether it is OK to play the Phrygian Dominant Bebop scale over the iim7b5 chord as well as the V7 chord. The answer is *absolutely*, although the theory as to why can seem a little intense on paper.

If you're anxious to get playing and skip the theory part, the 'too long, didn't read' answer is that the ii chord (Em7b5) functions as a suspended version of the A7 chord, almost in the same way that a Dsus4 chord resolves to D major. For this reason, it is fine to play A Phrygian Dominant over Em7b5. In fact, over 'quick' changes I'd highly recommend it!

The longer, slightly more complex answer is apparent when we look at the notes of Em7b5 *over* a bass note of A. As a slash chord, this can be written Em7b5/A

Example 8e shows which intervals the arpeggio notes of Em7b5 form when they are played over an A bass note.

Example 8e

The chord of Em7b5 can be seen as an A7b9sus4 chord.

Refer to Example 5f and you will see that the extended arpeggio we play on the A7 chord already contains the b9 note (Bb) note, so the only difference in this chord is that we have replaced the major 3rd of A7 with the 4th. We have created the chord A7b9sus4.

The suspended 4th in the A7b9sus4 (Em7b5) chord falls to the major 3rd on the chord V (A7). This means that we can now view our minor ii V i as the following progression. I have provided some chord voicings if you wish to play through these chords.

Example 8f

Look back at Example 6h. Notice how the arpeggio movement on the chord change mirrors the chord movement in the example above.

It follows that if we stick to our 'strong arpeggio notes on strong beats' approach, the Phrygian Dominant Bebop scale is extremely appropriate to use over the whole 'ii V' part of the progression.

In fact, if you want to you can continue with a normal (non-bebop) Phrygian dominant scale onto the tonic Dm7 chord as A Phrygian Dominant *is the same scale* as D Harmonic Minor. Just base your scale lines around the Dm7 arpeggio. D Harmonic Minor has a different bebop note though, so do be careful!

The take-away from all this theorising is that for most of the time, especially on a 'quick change' minor ii V i, we can effectively ignore the iim7b5 chord if we want. Of course, if you wish to articulate it go right ahead, but that approach is normally more suitable for 'long' changes at slower tempos.

Combining Arpeggios with the Phrygian Dominant Bebop Scale

The Phrygian Dominant Bebop scale is a very important part of the bebop repertoire. It is one of the fundamental building blocks of the jazz language so practicing it is essential study. For the rest of this chapter I will be treating the Em7b5 chord as an A7b9sus4 chord, i.e., ignoring it. Any clashes formed from playing the major 3rd (C#) against the D (Sus4) are momentary and not worth worrying about for now.

Example 9a

Example 9a begins on the 5th of the A7 (root of the Em7b5) and ascends the Phrygian Dominant Bebop scale, again targeting the 5th of A7. The line then descends the bebop scale resolving to the 5th of Dm7.

Play along with the slow backing track and analyse the line to see where the arpeggio notes fall. When you gain more confidence, move onto faster backing tracks. Take the same approach with all of the lines in this chapter.

Example 9b

This line begins on the major 3rd (C#) of the A7 chord and descends through the Phrygian Dominant Bebop scale targeting the b7 of A7 and the 5th of Dm7.

Example 9c

This melodic line targets the b7 of A7 and descends an arpeggio figure on the Dm7.

Example 9d

Here we target the root of A7 and the root of Dm7. Do you notice the D-C#-C movement on the Dm7 chord? This is taken from the D Aeolian Bebop scale which we will discuss in the next chapter.

Examine the following.

Example 9e

Example 9e shows that you do not *always* have to start on an arpeggio tone when using the bebop scale. You can always add in chromatic approach note to get yourself on to an arpeggio note on a strong beat.

In Example 9e, I begin on the b13 (F) which is definitely not an arpeggio tone. In order to hit an arpeggio tone on a strong beat I use the chromatic passing note F# to fill in the gap between F and G. This enables me to hit the b7 (G) of the A7 chord on beat two.

Notice that when I descend the similar sequence in bar two, I do not use this chromatic alteration because my chord tones are already on the beat.

See if you can find some other non-chord tones on which to begin your lines, then use chromaticism to help you return to the normal 'strong note on a strong beat' approach.

Now let's look at some Phrygian Dominant Bebop lines over quick minor ii V i changes.

Example 9f

Example 9f begins on the b7 of A7, ascends the Phrygian Dominant Bebop scale into the root of A before using an approach note pattern into the b3rd of Dm7.

Example 9g

In Example 9g I 'box in' the 3rd of A7 before targeting the root and descending to the minor 3rd of Dm7 where I ascend the 3-9 arpeggio.

45

Example 9h

In Example 9h I target the 3rd of A7 and use the bebop scale to target the 5th of Dm7 before using a common melodic pattern.

Example 9i

In this final example I ascend the A7 arpeggio (I was *thinking* 3-b9, but I don't actually reach the b9). Instead, I use the bebop note to approach the root of the A7 chromatically from below. I target the b3 of the Dm7 chromatically from above using the line G-F#-F.

As ever, it is acceptable that these lines contain many notes from outside our prevailing harmony, just so long as they are placed on weak beats and used to push our arpeggio notes onto strong beats.

The Aeolian Bebop Scale

The Aeolian Bebop scale was mentioned in the previous chapter and is extremely useful when it comes to soloing on the tonic minor 7 chord.

Remember that when we formed the minor ii V i, we changed the harmonically 'correct' min/Maj7 to be a *straight* m7 chord (which does not belong to the original harmonised parent key). It stands to reason that because this Dm7 chord does not belong in the Harmonic Minor scale, we need to use a different scale when soloing over the tonic chord.

*Big disclaimer: The Harmonic Minor scale does work very well over the Dm7 if you avoid playing the 7th note (C#) on a strong beat.

If you wish to create a Harmonic Minor Bebop scale, the formula is 1 2 b3 4 5 b6 (6) 7:

Explore the Harmonic Minor Bebop scale by yourself, but for now we will be discussing the Aeolian Bebop scale as I believe it to be a more accessible and appropriate sound to use in this context.

When we 'borrowed' the Dm7 tonic chord we took it from the Natural Minor (Aeolian) scale. This is the sixth mode of the F Major scale and is often referred to as the 'relative' minor scale.

The formula for the Aeolian scale is 1 2 b3 4 5 b6 b7 and it can be played like this on the guitar:

Example 10a

While this is a useful sound, and one you probably already know, it is more beneficial for us to immediately move on to learning the Aeolian Bebop scale for the reasons mentioned in the previous chapter.

The Aeolian Bebop scale is an eight-note scale formed by adding a natural 7 to the Aeolian Scale. The formula is 1 2 b3 4 5 b6 b7 (7).

The Aeolian Bebop scale in D can be played like this:

Example 10b

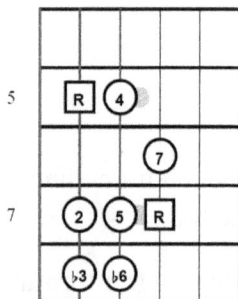

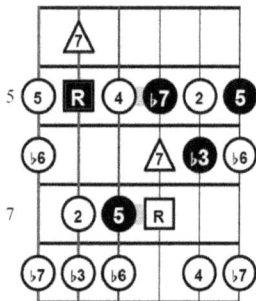

D Aeolian Bebop

As always, ascend and descend this scale beginning from the lowest root (D), ignoring to begin with all the lower notes in this fingering position. As you get used to the shape you may add in these lower notes. When you have memorised the scale shape, spend some practice time ascending or descending the scale from any of the Dm7 arpeggio notes (1 b3 5 or b7). This should satisfy you that wherever you start you will always keep the arpeggio tones on the beat when you play in 1/8th notes.

This bebop scale works in *exactly* the same way as the Phrygian Dominant Bebop scale you learned earlier.

Not only is the D Aeolian Bebop scale the 'correct' scale to play over the tonic Dm7 chord, there is another reason that the scale works so well. The note we have added to form this bebop scale is the *natural 7th* scale degree (C#). This note is the same as the *natural 7th* degree in the Harmonic Minor scale which is contained in chord V of the progression (C# is the 3rd of A7).

Compare the following two scale diagrams:

D Harmonic Minor   D Aeolian Bebop

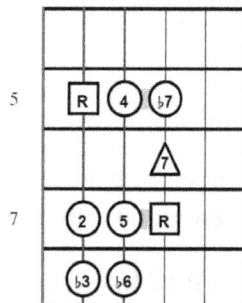

48

D Aeolian Bebop scale can be seen as *exactly* the same scale as D Harmonic Minor with the addition of one note.

The extra note is the b7 of the scale, which fits perfectly with the Dm7 chord we are playing in the harmony (formula 1 b3 5 **b7**).

At the same time, the natural 7th (C#) ties the melody together with the 'original' parent scale of the minor ii V i chord progression: the Harmonic Minor.

By using the Aeolian Bebop scale on the tonic Dm7 chord we are both acknowledging that the Dm7 chord has been altered from the original Harmonic Minor Dmin/Maj7 chord, while also carrying the natural 7th (C#) through from the ii V part of the progression. It is the best of both worlds.

Using the Aeolian Bebop Scale

The approach to applying the Aeolian Bebop scale melodically is the same as using the Phrygian Dominant Bebop Scale on the ii and V chords. As long as we start on a chord tone of Dm7 (1, b3, 5, or b7) we can ascend or descend the scale in any direction and the chord tones will remain on the beat.

Here are a few isolated examples:

Example 10c

Example 10c is a simple line that ascends from root to 5th.

Example 10d

Example 10d makes full use of the bebop scale moving from root to b7 twice before continuing to the b3.

Example 10e

Example 10e shows that you can use a chromatic approach note as well as the bebop scale. In this case I have used the G# to approach the 5th of Dm7. This idea works well as the G# is the 'bebop note' in the A Phrygian Dominant Bebop scale that you may have been using in the Em7b5 - A7 part of the chord progression.

Example 10f

Example 10f combines some melodic jumps with arpeggio figures.

It is important that you experiment and explore the D Aeolian Bebop scale and come up with your own favourite licks. The possibilities are almost limitless. Write down your best ideas and use them as resolutions to the minor ii V i progression. Use backing track 9 – a static Dm7 chord.

In the following examples I mainly use the Phrygian Dominant Bebop Scale on Em7b5 and A7 and switch to the Aeolian Bebop scale on Dm7.

I also freely combine arpeggios and chromatic approach notes with bebop scales while generally keeping the strong arpeggio tones on the strong beats of the bar.

This is a straightforward application of both bebop scales, but note the use of the D Minor Blues scale in the final bar.

Example 10g

Example 10h

In the first bar of Dm7 the melodic line ascends the Aeolian Bebop scale. In the second bar there is a common bebop phrase ending that you should know.

Example 10i

In Example 10i I don't target the A7 arpeggio in the first bar. Instead I target the Em7b5 arpeggio as you learned to do in the early chapters. Notice how this gives a subtly different effect.

Example 10j

Example 10j starts with an up-beat into bar one where I use a common chromatic approach note pattern.

When the ii V i changes are *slow* (one chord per bar), you have more time to target each individual chord i.e., make more of the Em7b5. However, when the chord changes are *fast*, (two chords per bar) it is often worth thinking A Phrygian Dominant Bebop for *both* the Em7b5 and A7, then switching to D Aeolian Bebop for the Dm7. This is shown below.

Example 10k

Useful Chord Voicings for the Minor ii V i Progression

To take a break from all the melodic theory, let's look at some useful ways to play and expand upon the actual minor iim7b5-V7-im7 chords in the progression.

The first things to consider are the available 'natural' tensions we can play on the V7 chord. Jazz musicians tend to agree that because the V7 is already the main point of tension in the chord progression, it is normally OK to add extra tension through extensions and chromatic alterations.

In the context of a minor ii V i progression, the *parent* scale of the V7 chord is the Phrygian Dominant scale (mode five of Harmonic Minor), as we have already seen.

The formula for the Phrygian Dominant scale is

1 b2 3 4 5 b6 b7.

If we remove the arpeggio notes from the scale (our basic '7' chord, 1 3 5 b7) we are left with the scale degrees b2, 4, b6.

~~1~~ b2 ~~3~~ 4 ~~5~~ b6 ~~b7~~

These notes, when added to chords or played an octave higher are named b9, 11 and b13 and are referred to as chord *extensions*. They can be added to our core A7 notes to add tension to the chord sound.

We often have to be careful when we add these extensions to chord voicings because they can cause an undesirable clash with the original chord tones. For example, the b6/b13 note is the same as a #5.

It is useful to see the b6/b13 as a #5 because it is immediately apparent that the #5 will clash with the natural 5 in the chord.

When we add a #5/b13 to a dominant 7 chord, we normally omit the natural 5 note to avoid the clash.

In the case of A7, we replace the natural 5th (E) with the #5/b13 (E#)

This can be seen easily here.

Example 11a:

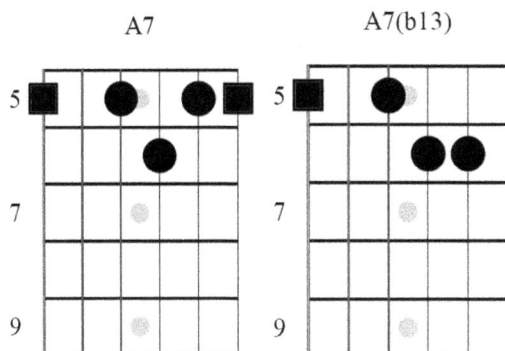

This is a great chord to play on the minor ii V i progression as the #5/b13 note becomes the b3 of the im7 chord. In this case the b13 in A7 is F, which becomes the b3 (F) in Dm7

Try it for yourself.

Example 11b

The same sort of principle applies to adding the b9. The b9 will clash with the root of the chord if it is placed next to it, so often a high octave root is replaced with the b9 while leaving the bass note unaltered.

Example 11c

It is often easier to finger the A7b9 chord if you only play the top four strings and leave the root note to the bass player.

Example 11d shows this approach in context:

You can also combine the b13 *and* the b9 as you can see here.

Example 11e

Again, most guitarists will not play the bass note of this chord voicing.

Example 11f shows this chord in context of the minor ii V i in D:

When playing the rhythm guitar part on a minor ii V i, all of the previous voicings can be used interchangeably on the V chord.

Drop 2 Voicings

Drop 2 chord voicings are an essential part of every jazz guitarist's vocabulary. Without delving too much into the theory of how they are created, they allow us to play any chord voicing on just the top four strings of the guitar, and by doing so they help us stay out of the way of other chordal instruments like the piano or organ.

They are extremely useful because they naturally lend themselves to good voice leading while giving us light, un-cumbersome chord voicings.

Any four note chord can be played in any one of four inversions ascending the guitar neck. Here are four useful ways to play the minor ii V i chord sequence Em7b5-A7-Dm7.

Example 11g

Example 11h

Example 11i

Em7b5   A7   Dm7

Example 11j

Em7b5   A7   Dm7

These chord voicing patterns should be memorised as they occur often in jazz. They also help you to 'see' how each individual note changes between chords. Have you noticed that only two notes change between Em7b5 and A7?

We can add any of the tensions previously discussed in this chapter to the V chord (A7). We simply need to know which notes to adjust in the voicing. The following four bars in Example 11k show how we can add interesting extensions to the A7 chord just by altering specific notes.

Example 11k:

A7   Root > b9   5 > b6   Combined examples

This can be done in all four of the previous inversions, so spend time investigating how to alter the A7 chord in each position. To get you started here are the same alterations in the next inversion.

Example 11l:

These chord voicings are used all the time and we often use more than one chord voicing on each chord. Doing so allows us to add melodic lines to chord voicings while comping, very much in the style of players like Joe Pass.

Playing Off the Relative Major

The concepts in this chapter were taught to me by my current teacher Pete Sklaroff, who is a wonderful jazz guitar player, teacher and friend. When he introduced me to these ideas I spouted a load of objections based around appropriate target notes and what I thought I knew about music theory… until he told me to relax and just play it. What resulted was a really bluesy sounding, 'hip' approach to soloing on the minor ii V I progression.

The theoretical concepts in the next few paragraphs are fairly complex, so once again the 'too long, didn't read' explanation is *play a Mixolydian Bebop Scale from the b3 of the dominant chord.*

Our dominant chord in the ii V i is A7. If we build a Mixolydian Bebop Scale from the b3 we generate the C Mixolydian Bebop Scale.

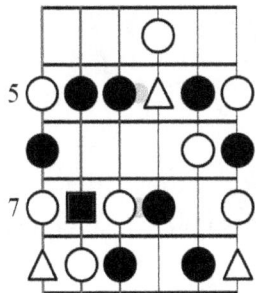

Example 12a

C Mixolydian Bebop

Dark dots = Em7b5 Arpeggio

Triangle dots = Root of C Mixolydian Bebop.

Try starting from any arpeggio note of Em7b5, (do not begin on the b7, D, replace it with the note C) and play the C Mixolydian Bebop scale over both Em7b5 *and* the A7 chords before resolving to a Dm7 arpeggio idea. You will hear a very 'hip' bluesy approach to soloing on these changes.

Let's take a deeper look at why this concept works with some tangible examples.

Relative Majors and Minors

The first important thing to understand about why the C Mixolydian Bebop scale works in this context is the concept of *relative major and minor keys*. In music there are always two possible key centres for any key signature: one major key and one *relative minor* key.

For example, if you see the key signature of C Major (no sharps or flats) at the start of a piece of music, then you know that the piece will *either* be in the key of C Major *or* A minor.

If you were to see the key signature of G Major, (1 sharp) you would know that the music is written in either the key of G Major or E minor.

The relative minor key is always built on the sixth degree of the major scale.

In other words, if you count up six notes from the major key you will find the relative minor. For example,

in the key of C count up, C D E F G A = A minor

In the key of G count, G A B C D E = E minor.

Another way to view this is that the relative minor key is always three semitones below the root of the major key.

Throughout this book we have been working in the key of D minor. The *relative major to D minor is F Major.*

Check: From the key of F Major, count up six notes: F G A Bb C D = D minor.

The musical link between the relative major and minor keys is *very* strong. If you play rock or blues guitar you may know that the notes of E Minor Pentatonic and G Major Pentatonic are the same. This is because G and E are relative major and minor.

3-9 Synonyms

The next thing to consider is which notes we play when we use the extended 3-9 arpeggios that were explored in Chapter Six.

When we build an extended 3-9 arpeggio from the D minor chord in the minor ii V i, we play the b3rd, 5th, b7th and 9th. These are the notes F, A, C and E. These notes form an *F Major 7th chord.*

When we build an extended 3-9 arpeggio from the Em7b5 chord in the minor ii V i, we play the b3rd, b5th, b7th and b9th. These are the notes G, Bb, D and F. These notes form a *G minor 7th chord.*

This can be seen more clearly in the following diagram:

Finally, when we play the extended 3-9 arpeggio from the A7 (V) chord we play the notes C#, E, G and Bb. These notes form a *rootless* C7b9 chord.

The chords/arpeggios we have created from using extended arpeggios are these:

Em7b5 = Gm7

A7 = C7b9

Dm7 = Fmaj7

The chords created by using extended arpeggios on a minor ii V i progression form a Major ii V I in the relative major key of F.

This is shown in Example 12b.

Example 12b:

Listen to and play Example 12b. Can you hear how strongly these two sounds are linked?

The third piece of the puzzle comes when you realise that the chords A7b9 and C7b9 contain *exactly the same notes when you omit the roots*. (Just like we did when we formed extended arpeggios).

Rootless A7b9 = C# E G Bb

Rootless C7b9 = E G Bb C#

You may already be aware that this is a 'diminished substitution' which leads to some very cool, *symmetrical scale* theory, but as we're already getting quite deep here I'll save that for another book!

Now we can see that not only do the major and minor ii V I's have a strong harmonic connection, the dominant (V) chords of both progressions share *exactly* the same tensions.

If we move back to viewing everything from the minor ii V i perspective for a minute, you will remember that we often treat the ii chord (Em7b5) as a suspended version of the V chord (A7b9). In simplistic terms, this means that we can effectively *ignore* the iim7b5 chord if we wish, especially at higher 'bop' tempos.

Summary

All the above points combined mean that a really effective way to solo over the first two chords of a minor ii V i progression is to imagine we're playing the dominant chord of the relative major ii V i. In this case, we are thinking C7.

As a general rule: on a minor ii V i, play a Mixolydian Bebop Scale a minor 3rd above the dominant chord.

The Mixolydian Bebop Scale

The C7 chord derives from major scale harmony (it is chord V of F Major), so the 'correct' scale to use is C Mixolydian, as it is the fifth mode in F Major. Its construction is 1 2 3 4 5 6 b7 and to form a bebop scale we add the natural 7th note giving us the formula 1 2 3 4 5 6 b7 7

Example 12a again for reference:

C Mixolydian Bebop

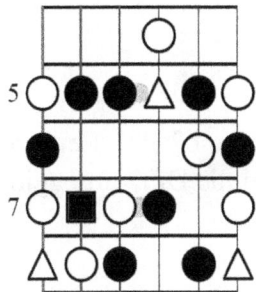

To help link the C Mixolydian Bebop Scale to the Em7b5 – A7b9 sound in the minor ii V i progression, *always begin your melodic line from an arpeggio note of Em7b5 but replace the b7 (D) with the root of the Bebop Scale (C).*

These notes are the solid dots in the fretboard diagram above.

Spend time learning the C Mixolydian Bebop scale over two octaves as shown here.

Example 12c

Using the Mixolydian Bebop Scale on Slow Changes

The golden rule is to begin your melodic line from an arpeggio note of Em7b5 except for the b7 (D). Replace it with the root of the Bebop scale (C). For now, we will resolve all of our lines to a note in the Dm7 arpeggio. We will often add chromatic approach notes to resolve smoothly.

Example 12d

This line descends the C Mixolydian Bebop scale from the b5 of the Em7b5 arpeggio and targets the #9 (C) of the A7 chord. The 5th of Dm7 is targeted with a chromatic passing note from below.

Example 12e

This line ascends from the root of Em7b5 and once again targets the #9 (C) of A7.

Example 12f

Descending from the root of the bebop scale (C), this melodic idea targets the b7 of the A7 chord with a chromatic approach note from below.

Example 12g

This sequential line descends the bebop scale from the root and targets the root of Dm7 with a fragment of the D Aeolian Bebop scale. In bar three there is an idea based around the D Minor Pentatonic scale.

Example 12h

Example 12h makes use of an ascending pattern throughout the C Mixolydian Bebop scale.

Example 12i

The final example utilises the Em7b5 arpeggio and the C Mixolydian Bebop scale to target the b9 in the A7 3-b9 arpeggio.

Using the Mixolydian Bebop Scale on Quick Changes

The C Mixolydian Bebop scale works extremely well over 'quick', two-beat minor ii V i's. Learn the following examples.

Example 12j

Example 12k

Example 12l

Example 12m

Playing the Mixolydian Bebop scale on the b3 of the dominant 7 chord is one of my favourite ways to approach soloing on a minor ii V i.

The Altered scale

The Altered scale or 'Super Locrian Mode' is the 7th mode of Melodic Minor and is extremely useful for adding tension to the dominant (V) chord in any ii V i progression.

It works so well because it contains all the important notes of a dominant 7 arpeggio (1, 3 and b7) plus *every* possible alteration to the chord: b9, #9, b5 and #5.

This is not immediately apparent when we first examine the scale formula, so let's take a quick look at the theory.

The Altered scale in the key of A (our dominant chord) is as follows:

In the left hand diagram, the Altered scale is written out according to its tradition scale formula:

1 b2 b3 b4 b5 b6 b7.

In the right hand diagram I have re-written the scale using the *enharmonic* spellings of some of the notes. Look at the b4 in the left hand diagram (Db). Db is the same as the note C#, and C# is the *major 3rd* of A7.

If I respell the b3 (C) in the left hand diagram as a B# that gives me a #2 degree, and by respelling the b6 (F) as a #5 (E#), the scale formula becomes

1 b2 #2 3 b5 #5 b7

Remember that when added as extensions to an arpeggio the b2 and #2 notes are renamed b9 and #9 so our scale for soloing purposes becomes

1 b9 #9 3 b5 #5 b7

This scale can now be seen as containing the 1, 3 and b7 from the dominant 7 arpeggio (the 5th is not important) plus all possible alterations to the dominant chord: b9, #9, b5 and #5.

The Altered scale has a dark, dissonant character which can be very musical if you approach it correctly. It also has a bit of inherent 'instability' due to its lack of a natural 5th.

When handled with care, the Altered scale is an extremely appropriate soloing choice over a minor ii V i because its b6 note becomes the b3 of the tonic minor chord as we saw in the chord voicings chapter.

In our minor ii V i in D the b6 in A7 is the note F and the b3 in Dm7 is also F.

As with every dominant scale choice so far, the Altered scale works well over both the iim7b5 and the V7 chord, although it does work 'better' over quick changes. Over slow changes there are some good scale options to use on the ii chord such as the Locrian Bebop Scale and the Locrian Natural 9 scale. Both of these will be discussed in later chapters.

For now we will focus on learning the resolutions from the A Altered scale to the Dm7 arpeggio. To begin with, learn the A Altered scale in two octaves as shown in **Example 13a.**

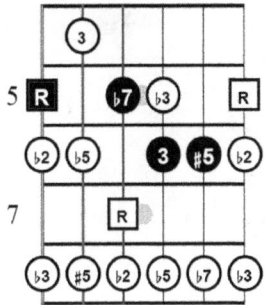

As we did earlier when we were first learning to hit chord changes, we will begin by focusing on very small areas of the neck, trying to find as many resolution points between A Altered and D minor 7 as we can. Initially, we will only play notes on the top two string group, using four notes from the Altered scale and resolving onto any arpeggio tone of Dm7.

Examples 13b–13e:

Now learn the resolutions points on the second and third strings. Some ideas are shown below.

Examples 13f–13i:

Repeat this process on all the other 2-string groups.

Initially, do these exercises freely with no metronome or backing track, but when you are confident of many of the resolutions, try working on these ideas with the A7b9b13 – Dm7 backing track (backing track 7). This may seem like a time consuming exercise, but the whole art to using the altered scale is to resolve it cleanly.

The next stage is to explore some 1/8th note lines over the 'quick' minor ii V i progression. Once again we will ignore the Em7b5 chord for now, treating it as an A7b9sus4 chord. Despite the Altered scale containing the note Eb (which we would expect to clash with the E natural in the Em7b5), this does work as an acceptable tension (b5) when viewed in terms of the A7 chord.

Try the following.

Examples 13j-13m:

The Altered Scale on Quick Changes

The Altered scale is very effective on 'quick' minor ii V i changes, especially at higher tempos where momentary dissonances over the iim7b5 chord are not as pronounced.

The Altered scale works well over slow changes too, especially at higher tempos as the next examples will show. I feel, however, that at slower tempos it is a much more effective approach to articulate the iim7b5 independently with related arpeggios and scales and only use the Altered scale on the V7.

For now, study the following ideas that use the Altered scale over slow minor ii V i changes on both the iim7b5 and the V chord.

Notice that I try to target what chord tones I can from Em7b5, and I treat both the #5 (E#) and b9 (Bb) as arpeggio tones on the A7b9b13 chord. This is because they are natural extensions and often played in the harmony parts with the root (A) and natural fifths (E) omitted.

The Altered Scale on Slow Changes

Example 13p

Example 13q

Example 13r

Example 13s

Once again, these are just a few ideas to get you started. The real benefit to your playing comes when you explore the scale by yourself, write your own lines and play along with the backing tracks. If some of the notes sound a little awkward at first, don't worry – this is just your musical ear developing. If in doubt, try playing your lines at a higher tempo and if you still don't like it, play something else.

You will find that most of the notes you find dissonant occur when the A Altered scale is played over the Em7b5 chord on slow changes at slower tempos.

Using the Min/Maj7 Arpeggio on the b9

One of the real benefits of using the Altered scale is that you can build a triad or arpeggio from *any* note of the Altered scale and it will sound great. This is true for *all* modes of the Melodic Minor scale and gives us a great deal of freedom when we want use arpeggios in our playing. I unfortunately don't have room here to go into massive depth on this subject, but I do want to share my favourite arpeggio substitution with you.

On a minor ii V i, my favourite arpeggio to use on the V chord is a min/Maj 7th on the b9.

If we are playing on an A7(altered) chord, this would be the arpeggio of Bbmin/Maj7.

The notes in Bb min/Maj7 are Bb, Db/C#, F and A.

These intervals when played over an A7 chord give us the intervals b9, 3, b13 and 1. Playing this arpeggio highlights the tension notes in the often used A7b9b13 chord. The arpeggio is shown in **Example 13t.**

73

Normally when using this arpeggio in this position I end up avoiding the two lowest notes on the guitar as they are a little cumbersome to play, although they do still sound great. Here are a few ideas that use the Bbmin/Maj arpeggio on the A7b9b13 chord.

Example 13u

Example 13v

Example 13w

In the previous examples I have targeted the arpeggio notes of Em7b5 in bar one using the Locrian Bebop scale (more on this in the next chapter), then used the Bb min/Maj7 arpeggio over the A7(altered) chord to hit the chord tones 1, b9, 3 and #5. Each time I resolve the A7 chord to a note from the Dm7 arpeggio.

As always, create and write your own lines and then speed them up with the backing tracks provided.

Backing tracks eight, nine and ten are 'slow change' minor ii V i progressions in D with an A7b9b13 chord as the dominant chord.

The Locrian Mode on iim7b5

When we have more time to solo on each chord, for example over slow (one bar per chord) changes it can be desirable (and easier!) to play more articulately over the Em7b5 chord.

We can use the 'arpeggio and approach note' technique as already discussed, or we can use an appropriate scale. There are two main scale choices we can use on the Em7b5 chord, and the first one we will look at is the Locrian mode.

Locrian is the seventh mode of the Major scale, and you will probably already know that when harmonised, the 7th degree of the Major scale forms a m7b5 chord. As the Locrian mode is built around a m7b5 chord it is perfect to use when soloing on the iim7b5.

The formula for the Locrian mode is **1** b2 **b3** 4 **b5** b6 **b7**

Although we will learn the E Locrian mode around an Em7b5 chord, it is very helpful to know that it contains *exactly* the same notes as D Aeolian, which is the scale we are currently using to resolve all our melodic ideas.

Here's the E Locrian mode.

Example 14a

E Locrian

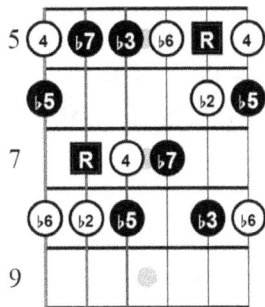

To form the more useful Locrian Bebop scale, we add a natural 7th (D#) between the b7 (D) and root (E). While the notes of the seven note E Locrian scale are the same as the D Aeolian mode, the bebop note is different so we need to learn a slightly different scale pattern.

Here's how you play the Locrian Bebop scale.

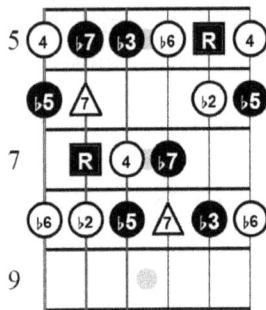

Examples 14b

E Locrian Bebop

Once again, as with any bebop scale, if you start on an arpeggio tone (shown with dark dots) and play in a scalic fashion, you will always hit an arpeggio tone on the beat. From now on in this chapter we will be working with the Locrian Bebop scale.

Remember that it contains the same notes as D Aeolian but the 'bebop note' has moved.

We will begin by learning some E Locrian Bebop scale lines which resolve onto arpeggio tones of the A7b9 chord. I am giving you full one-bar lines here, but as always it is best to split your guitar into two-string groups and explore the changes over small areas.

Example 14c begins on the root of E Locrian Bebop and targets the b9 of the A7 chord.

Examples 14c

Example 14d descends E Locrian Bebop scale from b3 and descends the A Phrygian Dominant Bebop.

Examples 14d

Example 14e targets the b7 of the A7 before combining a 3-b9 extended arpeggio with a Bbmin/Maj arpeggio.

Examples 14e

Example 14f descends from the b5 of the Em7b5 chord and descends the Phrygian Dominant Bebop scale from the 3rd of A7.

Examples 14f

Melodic Sequences Using Three Different Scales

Now we can use different eight-note scales on each chord, one idea we can examine is to take a *melodic sequence* through the whole progression. This is a very strong approach to take when soloing on changes if used sparingly.

Study the ideas in the following examples to find the melodic sequences. Each example uses the Phrygian Dominant Bebop Scale, but do feel free to experiment with any dominant scale choice on the V chord.

Example 14g

The previous example revolves around a descending/ascending Bebop Scale pattern, targeting the closest arpeggio tone on each change.

Example 14h

In Example 14h, I ascend five arpeggio notes before descending the appropriate scale.

Example 14i

This example descends five scale notes before ascending the arpeggio and places a scale tone on the last note of the bar, targeting a chord tone in the next.

Example 14j

The first two beats in each bar of Example 14j use an arpeggio/scale approach note pattern into beat three before descending a scale/arpeggio figure.

Patterns like these are fun to write and play. They are virtually limitless in their possibilities and whole books have been written on their formation. They're an extremely strong, articulate melodic device.

The Locrian Natural 9 Mode

The Locrian Natural 9 (or Locrian Natural 2) mode is the *sixth* mode of the Melodic Minor scale.

Unfortunately, I do not have room in this book to discuss a great deal of Melodic Minor scale theory, but in the same way that the *seventh* chord of the Major Scale harmonises to form a 4-note m7b5 chord, the same is true of chord *six* of the Melodic Minor scale.

Continuing to work with the chord *Em7b5* we need to find which Melodic Minor scale has the note 'E' as its sixth degree.

The scale of G Melodic Minor has the note E as its sixth degree as you can see in the following diagram:

(Technically this key signature is incorrect but this makes the scale much easier to read).

If we rearrange this scale to make the note 'E' the root, then we have created the E Locrian Natural 9 mode.

The arpeggio notes E, G, Bb and D are bracketed. As you can see, the chord formed from the root of the scale is an Em7b5. You should also notice that every note in the scale, except for the natural 2nd (or 9th, F#) is the same as in the E Locrian mode that we explored in the previous chapter.

It is the natural 9th (F#) in Locrian Natural 9 as opposed to the b9 (F) in Locrian that makes a huge difference to the sound and feel of the scale.

The Locrian Natural 9 mode can be played in the following way on the guitar:

Example 15a

E Locrian Nat 9

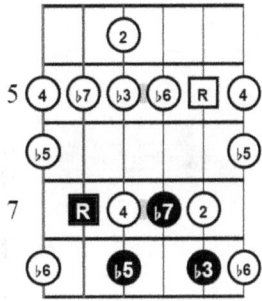

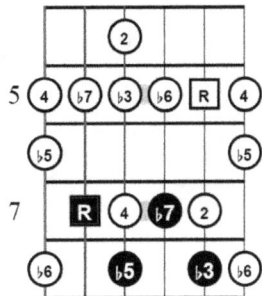

Learn this scale from the root, E while visualising the Em7b5 chord you already know.

As this is a seven note scale, it is extremely useful to add an eighth 'bebop' note. Once again, this note lies between the b7 and root. The Locrian Natural 9 Bebop scale is an extremely useful sound in jazz.

Example 15b

E Locrian Nat 9

In the fretboard diagram, the Locrian Natural 9 scale is shown built around the notes of an Em7b5 arpeggio.

Once you have learned this scale, play ascending and descending lines beginning from any Em7b5 arpeggio note to help you internalise the fact that playing the scale in 1/8th notes from an arpeggio tone will always land you on an arpeggio tone on a strong beat.

Do this over a static Em7b5 chord (backing track 8) to get your ears used to the natural 9 note. You may wish to treat this exercise as not just simply learning a new scale – you could view it as playing a 'normal' E Locrian scale and raising the 2nd degree each time. Some examples are given below.

Examples 15c

Examples 15d

Examples 15e

Example 15f

If the Locrian Natural 9 scale is a new sound for you, take some time here to write and play your own original lines. Make sure you target chord tones on the beats and let the other scale tones fall on the off beats.

When using the Locrian Natural 9 scale on the ii chord, my natural preference seems to be towards the Altered scale on the V chord. Try various options and see which your personal favourite is. Here are some minor ii V i lines which use Locrian Natural 9 and then shift to various different scales on the V chord.

Example 15g

Example 15g descends the Locrian Natural 9 Bebop scale and targets the major 3rd of the A7 chord before climbing the Bb min/Maj7 arpeggio and descending the Altered scale to the b3 of the Dm7 chord.

Example 15h

In Example 15h, I use a chromatic passing (bebop) note to target the root of the A7 chord. I then descend the Phrygian Dominant Bebop scale to land on the 5th of the D minor.

Example 15i

Again, beginning with the Locrian Natural 9 Bebop Scale, I consciously use the same melodic shape throughout the Em7b5 and A7 chords. I resolve the line to the b7 of the D Aeolian Bebop scale.

Example 15j

Example 15j is a line written in the lower octave with a great deal of chromaticism created by linking together bebop scales. Here I target the b7 of the Phrygian Dominant Bebop scale on the V chord.

The Melodic Minor Scale

Thus far, we have only looked at using one scale on the tonic chord: the Aeolian scale. Another commonly used option is the Melodic Minor scale. As we have now looked at using modes of the Melodic Minor scale on both the ii and the V chord, it is now appropriate to study the Melodic Minor scale on the i chord.

While the Melodic Minor as a resolution point for the minor ii V i can be a bit of an 'acquired taste', understanding its theory and application does allow us to access one of the most useful and strong melodic devices that musicians use on a minor ii V i.

The Melodic Minor scale contains the intervals:

1 2 b3 4 5 6 7

In the key of D minor, that gives us the notes shown in here.

Example 16a

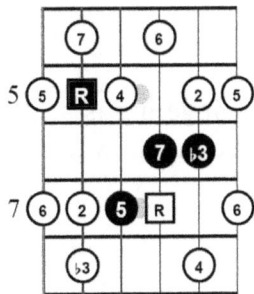

D Melodic Minor

You will immediately see two big differences between the Melodic Minor scale and the Aeolian mode that we have been using until now. The Melodic Minor scale does *not* contain a b7 and *does* contain a Natural 6th.

Thinking back to the formation of the minor ii V i progression, the original parent scale was the Harmonic Minor scale, which does contain a natural 7 degree, so our ear will accept the note if we use it on an off-beat.

The natural 6th (B) is a little more dissonant to our ears when you consider that until now we have been using the note Bb on both the ii and V chords. However, when I've raised questions like this, the answer has always been the same: "You just have to commit to the idea. If you play it strongly and with good time your phrasing will make it work."

This is good advice in all walks of life, but especially in music. Commit to what you're doing and play it with confidence.

One of the things that can really help to carry the natural 6th in the Melodic Minor is to add a b6 bebop note. Doing this in effect makes us treat the natural 6th as a chord tone by placing it on a strong beat. It also pushes the natural 7th onto the off-beat which helps combat the clash between the b7 in the Dm7 chord and the natural 7 in the scale.

By doing this we're giving a lot of attention to the natural 6th, but this can work really well.

Study and learn the D Melodic Minor Bebop Scale. The notes that are played on the beats (1, b3, 5, and 6) are highlighted.

Example 16b

Learn this scale thoroughly and play it over a static Dm7 chord (backing track 9). The fingering is a little awkward, so go slowly and get it right before moving on to learning the scale in two octaves as shown.

Example 16c

D Melodic Minor Bebop

To get you started, we will study some strong melodic ideas based around the Melodic Minor Bebop scale. All these ideas can be played on the tonic chord of any minor ii V i lick you know.

Try the following examples over backing track 9 – a static Dm7 chord.

Example 16d is a simple idea descending from the 5th.

Example 16d

Example 16e descends and then ascends from the root of Dm7

Example 16e

Example 16f is a semi sequential line descending from the 6th.

Example 16f

Example 16g is a longer line ascending from the root to the 6th with a classic bebop ending.

Example 16g

In Example 16h you ascend from the b3 of Dm7 and finally, in Example 16i, we take a semi sequential scale idea from the 5th up to the b3.

Example 16h

Example 16fi

As always, the more time you spend studying this scale, writing lines and jamming with different speed backing tracks, the more insight you will have into its sound and feel. This scale shape can be somewhat awkward so treat the tablature only as a suggested fingering. If you find your own way to play these lines, your phrasing will change and you will develop your own musical identity.

The following lines are all full minor ii V i phrases that use a variety of different approaches on the first two chords, but all resolve to the D Melodic Minor Bebop scale.

Example 16j

Example 16k

Example 16l

Example 16m

Here are a couple of lines for 'short' ii V i's using the same approach.

Example 16n

Example 16o

The Melodic Minor scale can certainly be an acquired taste at first, but stick with it and soon that natural 6th will be comfortable in your ears. Being able to use Melodic Minor in this way opens the door to some very exciting approaches or 'tricks' you can use to form strong, sequential movements up the guitar neck.

All will become clear in the next chapter.

The Best Trick in the Book: Moving Lines in Thirds

If you go back and revise the chapter on the Locrian Natural 9 mode, you will see that the *parent* scale of E Locrian Natural 9 is **G Melodic Minor**. (*E Locrian Natural 9 is mode six of G Melodic Minor*).

You will also remember that the A Altered scale is the 7th mode of **Bb Melodic Minor**.

An extremely strong melodic approach to soloing over Em7b5 – A7 is to *think* G Melodic Minor moving to Bb Melodic Minor.

You should remember that the extended 3-9 arpeggio for Em7b5 formed a **Gm7** chord, and that we can use a **Bbmin/Maj7** arpeggio to outline some tasty notes from the A Altered scale. Listen to **Example 17a:**

Even though I am simply playing up through the two melodic minor scales, you can hear the same tensions you have been playing when you used the E Locrian Natural 9 and the A Altered scale.

To reiterate: G Melodic Minor contains all the notes of E Locrian Natural 9, and Bb Melodic Minor contains all the notes of the A Altered scale.

The *distance* between the notes G and Bb is a *minor 3rd*.

This means that we can play any strong G Melodic Minor line over Eb7m5 and simply shift it up a b3rd (3 frets) to play a Bb Melodic Minor line. This is an *extremely* common approach to playing over a minor ii V. To make things simple, let's use the low fingering of G Melodic Minor

Example 17b:

G Melodic Minor

We will begin by working with a 'slow' minor ii V i to help illustrate this concept. First, I will form a line from G Melodic Minor:

Example 17c

Now I will simply shift this idea up three frets so it becomes a Bb Melodic Minor / A Altered Line:

Example 17d

To resolve the line, I can simply target the closest note in a Dm7 arpeggio. However, as we will see shortly, we can shift this pattern again to play a D Melodic Minor scale.

Here are some examples of the b3 translation approach to soloing on Em7b5 to A7(altered).

Examples 17e-17h

In the previous four examples, I take a sequence from the G Melodic Minor (E Locrian Natural 9) scale and simply shift it up three frets into a Bb Melodic Minor (A Altered) line. As you can see, the first note in the A7 bar is always three frets above the first note in the Em7b5 bar.

Our rule is this:

Play a Melodic Minor line from the b3 of the ii chord. Shift your line up three frets for the V chord.

Or you could simply play Locrian Natural 9 on the ii chord and then move up three frets on the V chord.

I really enjoy sliding up the guitar neck in this way. To me, the general direction of the ii V i chords always seems to be descending. Using the methods described in this chapter we are easily able to create *contrary* ascending motion in our solos.

Resolving to the Melodic Minor Scale

So far you have resolved these translated melodic minor lines as you have seen fit. However, we will now resolve the lines to D Melodic Minor using a similar, powerful concept.

We are currently playing the Bb Melodic Minor scale over the A7 chord. *The scale of D Melodic Minor is a major 3rd above the scale of Bb Melodic Minor.*

Any Bb Melodic Minor line can be shifted up a **major 3rd** (4 frets) to become a D Melodic Minor line.

We can see this in action in **Example 17i.**

Listen to, and play through the previous example with a backing track to get a feel for this concept.

Try out the following minor ii V i line using the '3rds' concept.

Example 17j

This line starts off in the same way as Example 17d, but on the Dm7 chord I shift the A7 line up a major 3rd. (In other words, the first note on Dm7 is four frets above the first note on A7).

This major 3rd upward shift will always resolve your minor ii V i lines when you use the Altered scale on chord V, and is a lot stronger if it preceded by the minor 3rd shift from Em7b5 to A7.

The rule we have created is now this:

Play a melodic minor line from the b3 of the iim7b5 chord. Move that line up a b3rd for the V7 chord. To resolve the phrase, move the line up a major 3rd to play the tonic melodic minor.

To internalise this important concept, try resolving examples 17e-17h by shifting the A7 phrase up a major 3rd.

The first one is done for you

Example 17k

Of course, you don't have to start your pattern on the 'same' note when you shift position. Here are some lines that still shift in the way we have studied, but they move more smoothly from one position to another.

Example 17l

Example 17m

Changing Keys and Longer Solos

As you are probably aware, jazz chord progressions are rarely static and often change key centres many times in the space of just a few bars. While it is an important goal to be able to change key (via targeting appropriate arpeggio notes) in any position on the guitar, for now we can focus on a few useful techniques to transpose the ideas we already know into new keys by simply changing position on the neck.

The secret is to learn all our lines and patterns starting from specific arpeggio notes in relation to a chord voicing.

As an example, look at the following chord progression. It consists of two minor ii V i progressions. The first is in the key of D minor, and the second is in the key of F minor.

We will use the following lick to solo over these chord changes.

Example 18a

This line begins on the note 'G' which is the b3 of the Em7 chord. Make sure you can play it from memory.

Now let's remind ourselves of how the Em7b5 chord and arpeggio lie on the guitar:

Em7b5 Arpeggio

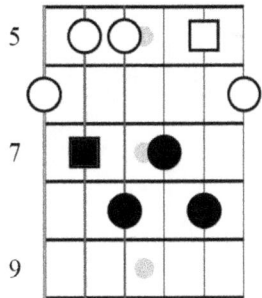

As you can see, the lick in Example 18a begins from a chord note, the solid dot on the second string. Visualise this chord as you play the first eight notes of the line.

Knowing where this line begins in relation to the chord we are visualising helps us when we change key centres. All we have to do is translate the chord shape and start our lick from the same chord tone. We will automatically play the same line in a different key. It's just like moving barre chords.

Play the above chord at the 10th fret on your guitar. It is now a Gm7b5. Play the same lick again, but now translate it up the neck so it begins on the equivalent note on the Gm7b5 chord (second string, eleventh fret).

Example 18b

When you can play through this line in the new position, play both 18a and 18b with backing track 10 as shown.

Example 18c

Using this method we can easily learn to target the changes.

Try **Example 18d:**

This lick begins from the root of the Em7b5 chord and uses the Phrygian Dominant Bebop scale. When you have it memorised, try transposing it so it is a minor ii V i lick in the key of F minor as we did before.

Try not to 'cheat' and look at the answer in the following example unless you really need to. Simply visualise the line starting from the root of your m7b5 chord shape and slide the chord up the neck to the 10th fret: Gm7b5.

Example 18e

Now for something a little trickier: Let's use the line from *18d for the ii V i in D* and the line from *18a to solo over the ii V i in F minor.*

Example 18f

As you can see, by combining different lines in this way you can use different licks over each set of chord changes. It's a great way to combine different soloing concepts too. Over one ii V i you might use an Altered scale idea, on another you might use a Mixolydian Bebop line from the b3 of the dominant. This will keep your playing fresh, interesting and full of new sounds.

My suggestion is to initially learn or write two licks for each arpeggio note of the Em7b5 chord (1 b3 b5 b7), one ascending and one descending. This gives you a minimum of eight lines to play for a ii V i.

I have selected some lines as a good starting points for you here, but feel free to choose your favourites from the book. Even better: write your own licks, so your playing is unique and expressive of *your* own musical voice.

(The previous line begins from the 3rd of A7).

Over quick / short changes you may wish to learn your lines around the arpeggio/chord shape for the dominant chord as we normally view the ii(m7b5) chord as a suspended dominant as we have previously seen.

By taking this approach you will learn to mix many different musical concepts when you solo on different minor ii V i chord progressions. The best thing is that your lines will naturally start to combine with each other and become unique to you. Your ears will start to guide you and you can dispense with licks altogether.

The lines in this book are not "*The Licks*" you must know. They are simply my demonstrations of how to apply different melodic concepts on the guitar in one position. We haven't even *mentioned* rhythm yet!

My advice to you is to treat everything you read and play in this book as ear training. Only by developing our ears can we gain access to what it is we truly wish to express.

Application to Different Positions of the Guitar Neck

I firmly believe that leaning to solo over jazz chord changes in one position on the neck is the quickest and most efficient way to getting a good and articulate melodic repertoire. Not only does it teach you the concepts, it also trains your ears to hear them and to be able to produce them unconsciously. Removing all the possible distractions of the different positions on the guitar neck keeps us focused and driven towards our goals.

When you are ready to explore other positions on the guitar neck, I recommend choosing a different key to work in. In this chapter I will give you all the tools you need to apply the concepts to a *minor ii V i in G minor*, but it is your job to apply it. You will learn more this way than any book can ever teach you.

Here, the ii(m7b5) chord is located on the sixth string, the V(7) chord is on the fifth string and the tonic is located on the sixth string.

As ever, the tablature fingerings are only suggestions. Go slowly and internalise one idea before moving on.

The previous few pages may look quite daunting, but there is nothing here that you haven't already covered in a different neck position earlier in this book. I would suggest that you work through the whole book again, but replace the earlier scales and arpeggios with the ones listed here instead.

Conclusions and Takeaways

There is a colossal amount of information in this book that has taken me years to study and incorporate into my playing. I use some ideas more than others and I certainly have my favourites.

One thing that most students seem to forget when learning to play solo jazz guitar is that the melody should inspire the solo. Too many musicians finish playing the head of the tune and then treat the next 32 bars as a blank canvas to show off all their licks. This is not a musical approach to jazz guitar soloing.

The first step to learning a tune is to do just that: LEARN THE TUNE! Then learn the chords. Your solos will greatly benefit from having the melody strongly in your ears, as not only will you have a melody you can simply embellish, you will also already have the strong target notes of the song in your head.

If you're playing a jazz standard, why not learn the words and sing it as you play it. This will help you deeply internalise the melody, chords and the form, helping you to never get 'lost' in the changes.

Knowing the tune inside and out will also guide you towards the most appropriate soloing concepts to use. If the song has been heavily emphasising Phrygian Dominant, do you really think the best thing to do is to immediately start using Altered scale ideas?

There are no rights or wrongs because music is subjective, but my tendency would be to solo using the scales from which the song is constructed at first, before moving on to more harmonically distant concepts in later choruses.

Also, know your genre. The bebop approach is strongly based around appropriate arpeggios with chromatic approach notes. Other forms of jazz are less so. Your ears, not your fingers are your best friend here: listen to how various different musicians approach the song you are learning. Try transcribing a chorus or just a lick or two.

It is better to have one concept strongly mastered than to spend your time trying to keep ten different plates spinning. When it's time to solo you will play your lines with confidence and good time. Thinking about all the different possibilities you *could* be using distracts you from your one and only aim: expression.

Commit to the idea. It's better to play a couple of 'wrong' notes in a confident solo than 100 weak, unassured, inarticulate notes because you're over-thinking. Believe me, I suffered from this for years. If in doubt, keep it simple and *commit to the idea.*

Some good minor ii V i tunes to get you started are:

Softly as in a Morning Sunrise, Alone Together, and *Stella by Starlight*

My best piece of advice is to apply any new soloing concept to a real tune as soon as you possibly can. This will make the theory come alive and help you to internalise each sound in a realistic environment. If you only learn a concept in isolation, you will find that the idea is hard to 'trigger' in a live performance situation. Get used to these ideas while playing real music.

Have fun.

Other Books from Fundamental Changes

Chord Tone Soloing for Jazz Guitar

Complete Technique for Modern Guitar

Fundamental Changes in Jazz Guitar

Guitar Chords in Context

Guitar Finger Gym

Guitar Fretboard Fluency

Guitar Scales in Context

Jazz Blues Soloing for Guitar

Jazz Guitar Chord Mastery

Minor ii V Mastery for Jazz Guitar

Sight Reading Mastery for Guitar

The Circle of Fifths for Guitarists

The Complete Guide to Playing Blues Guitar Compilation

The Complete Jazz Guitar Soloing Compilation

The First 100 Jazz Chords for Guitar

The Jazz Guitar Chords Compilation

The Melodic Minor Cookbook

The Practical Guide to Modern Music Theory for Guitarists

Voice Leading Jazz Guitar

100 Classic Jazz Licks for Guitar

Modern Jazz Guitar Concepts with Jens Larsen

Martin Taylor Beyond Chord Melody